Manual
224 Benefit Street
Providence, RI 02903
United States
Manual@risd.edu
risdmuseum.org

Issue — 6 / Spring 2016 / *Assemblage*
RISD Museum director: John W. Smith
Manual Editor-in-chief: Sarah Ganz
Blythe with S. Hollis Mickey
Editor: Amy Pickworth
Graphic designer: Derek Schusterbauer
Photographer: Erik Gould (unless
otherwise noted)
Printer: GHP

Special thanks to Emily Banas, Denise
Bastien, Gina Borromeo, A. Will
Brown, Laurie Brewer, Linda Catano,
Sionan Guenther, Jan Howard, Kate
Irvin, Dominic Molon, Ingrid Neuman,
Maureen C. O'Brien, Emily Peters,
Alexandra Poterack, Glenn Stinson,
Jessica Urick, and Elizabeth A. Williams.

This issue of *Manual* is supported in
part by a grant from the Rhode Island
State Council on the Arts, through
an appropriation by the Rhode Island
General Assembly and a grant from
the National Endowment for the
Arts. It is also made possible by the
Andrew W. Mellon Foundation in support of Assemblages, a collaboration
between the Haffenreffer Museum
of Anthropology at Brown University
and the RISD Museum at the Rhode
Island School of Design focusing on
the new and evolving field of object-
based teaching and research. Additional generous support is provided
by the RISD Museum Associates and
Sotheby's.

*Manual: a journal about art and i[ts]
making* (ISSN 2329-9193) is prod[uced]
twice yearly by the RISD Museum.
Contents © 2016 Museum of Art, Rhode
Island School of Design

Manual is available at RISD WORKS
(risdworks.com) and as a benefit of
RISD Museum membership. Learn more
at risdmuseum.com. Back issues can be
found online at issuu.com/risdmuseum.
Funds generated through the sales of
Manual support educational programs
at the RISD Museum.

Issue — 6

(cover and inside cover)
Pepón Osorio
Puerto Rican, b. 1955
T.K.O., 1989
Stainless steel utensils, cardboard, decals,
PVC figurines, plastic sunglasses, Mylar, metal
toy cars, boxing gloves, fabric, paint, and glue in a
wooden box covered in red velvet and white lace
34.3 × 37.5 × 28.3 cm. (13 ½ × 14 ¾ × 11 ⅛ in.) (open)
Helen M. Danforth Acquisition Fund 2001.30
© Pepón Osorio

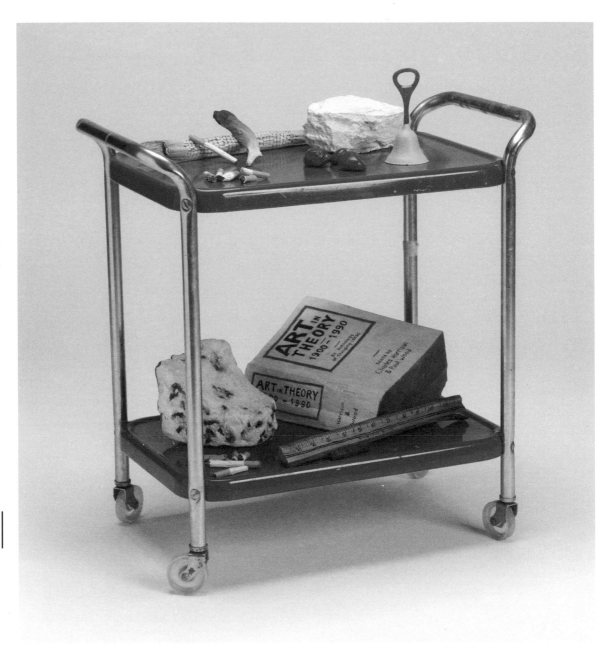

Leidy Churchman
American, b. 1979
Cart in Theory, 2008
Oil on wood, rocks, and bell on a found metal cart
55.9 × 54.6 × 30.5 cm. (22 × 21½ × 12 in.)
Lippitt Acquisition Fund 2011.18
Courtesy of the artist and Murray Guy, New York

Eric Anderson is an assistant professor of art history at RISD, where he teaches courses on modern design. His current research focuses on the psychology of design in nineteenth-century Vienna.

Taylor Elyse Anderson is a graduate student at the Fashion Institute of Technology in New York. In 2015 she was a Mellon Foundation summer intern with RISD Museum's Costume and Textiles Department, where she began her master's thesis research on early 20th-century textile subscription firms.

Bob Dilworth creates assemblages and works on canvas and paper that have been exhibited throughout the United States and collected by museums and corporations. A RISD graduate (BFA 1973, Painting), he is a professor in the Department of Art and Art History at the University of Rhode Island, where he teaches painting, drawing, design, and African American art history.

Christina Hemauer and Roman Keller, collaborators since 2003, are a Switzerland-based duo focusing on the amalgamation of physical and cultural realities. In 2006 they proclaimed a new era in art history: Postpetrolism.

Mariani Lefas-Tetenes is the assistant director for school and teacher programs at the RISD Museum, where she manages K–12 school visits and teacher professional development workshops, and coordinates the development of resources for students and teachers.

Simone Leigh is a professor in RISD's Ceramics and Graduate Studies departments. Her sculpture is included in the Greater New York 2015 exhibition at PS 1/MoMA. Her solo exhibition *I ran to the rock to hide my face the rock cried out no hiding place* opened in February 2016 at Artspace in Kansas City, Missouri.

Leora Maltz-Leca is an associate professor of contemporary art history at RISD, where she teaches courses on global contemporary art and critical theory. She is the author of *William Kentridge: Process as Metaphor & Other Doubtful Enterprises* (University of California Press, 2017) and is currently working on a second book, *The Metaphoric Studio: Material Politics in and Out of the Postcolonies.*

Ingrid A. Neuman is the sculpture conservator at the the RISD Museum. In addition to the examination, stabilization, and treatment of sculptures, she enjoys teaching RISD students about the selection of art materials and their interaction with environmental factors. The Buddha project provided her with a unique opportunity to explore art-making practices in Japan.

Tara Nummedal is an associate professor of history at Brown University, where her teaching and research explore the knowledge of nature and its place in the society and culture of early modern Europe. The author of *Alchemy and Authority in the Holy Roman Empire* (University of Chicago Press, 2007), she is currently writing a book about alchemist Anna Zieglerin and the intersection of science, gender, and religious culture in Reformation Germany.

Todd Oldham is best known as a clothing, product, and interior designer. His innovative bricolage approach earned him an honorary doctorate degree from RISD in 2014, and his work is the focus of *All of Everything: Todd Oldham Fashion*, on view at the RISD Museum through September 11, 2016.

Britany Salsbury is the Andrew W. Mellon Curatorial Fellow in the Department of Prints, Drawings, and Photographs at the RISD Museum. She recently completed a PhD dissertation on print series in fin-de-siècle Paris, and is currently working on an exhibition about etching during that period.

Table of Contents

Spring 2016

Manual

Assemblage

A metallic dollar sign swinging from a pair of boxing gloves, a plastic head of garlic, toy cars and soldiers hidden behind fake leaves—these are all affixed to the top of the box. The interior, lined in red velvet and trimmed in lace, is part picnic basket, part jewelry box, part candy sampler. Arranged in rows are shiny switchblades and less dangerous utensils embellished with diminutive globes, keys, Catholic iconography, photographs of culpable political figures, wedding-cake brides and grooms, and plastic ferns and bibles, skeletons and pigs. Readymade and handmade, utilitarian and unusable, the evidence of play beside violence made decorative, this lively assemblage is Pepón Osorio's *T.K.O.*, featured on the cover and interior. Its name refers to "technical knock-out," the term used to describe a boxing match ended when one participant cannot safely continue to fight. Each element in Osorio's arrangement, plucked from its usual contexts and animated through ad-hoc connections, fights for attention while playing nice, pulling a collective punch.

An assemblage is both act and result—the gathering and conjoining as well as the state of having been gathered and conjoined. This issue of *Manual* pieces together works made out of practical necessity and others that marry dazzling embellishments for optimal effect, examining how history (or one version of it) was (and is) pastiched from disparate sources, how fashionable textile samples were collected, and more (always more). An assembly of assemblages, an assortment of intended and unintended interrelationships, *Manual* issue six is the sum of its parts and the parts themselves, a dynamic gathering of artists and authors, objects and interpretations, mash-ups and remixes, lemons and lightbulbs, vibrantly interanimating each other.

Columns

From the Files pries open the archive, Double Take looks at one object two different ways, Artist on Art offers a creative response by an invited artist, Object Lesson exposes the stories behind objects, Portfolio presents a series of objects on a theme, How To explores the making of an object

From the Files

Object:	Scrapbook of Textile Ribbon Samples, ca. 1903	Dimensions:	35.6 x 25.4 x 11.4 cm. (14 x 10 x 4 1/2 in.)
Textile Distributor:	J. Claude Frères et Cie, Paris	Acquisition:	Gift of C. Alphonse Haus / Empire Silk Company INV2004.260
Materials:	Silk swatches mounted on paper and bound in leather		

Assembling Trends: A 1903 Sample Book
by Taylor Elyse Anderson

In the nineteenth and twentieth centuries, much like today, Paris was perhaps the most concrete authority in the world of fashion. Creative personnel in the design industry looked to Paris for trends and inspiration. For textile manufacturers, roles were clear: Paris set the standards, and mills outside of France aimed to supply their own market according to these demands.[1]

By the 1830s, firms were offering subscription services in which they assembled and sent textile-swatch representations of on-trend Parisian styles—as well as cutting-edge weave techniques and constructions—to foreign textile mills.[2] Upon arrival, mill staff would compile the fabrics into volumes according to firm, date, and/or season, gluing various swatches to the large paper pages of leather-bound books.[3]

The RISD Museum's Costume and Textiles Department owns thousands of these fabric swatches, gifts from local textile mills that once subscribed to these Parisian firms. Although many swatches are mounted on archival rag board and stored in banker's boxes, some remain in their original sample-book layout, collaged and glued to the same paper for more than a century. These brittle pages tell the story of various techniques, various countries, and various artists. Through sample books like this one, we are given a glimpse into the world of the American textile designer seeking inspiration, the Parisian agent sifting through trends, and the European socialite, donning the latest fashions on the French streets.

9
⁄
68

Issue—6

1 Diane Fagan Affleck, *Just New from the Mills: Printed Cottons in America, Late Nineteenth and Early Twentieth Centuries* (North Andover, Massachusetts: Museum of American Textile History, 1987), 30.
2 Regina Lee Blaszczyk, *The Color Revolution* (Cambridge, Massachusetts: MIT Press, 2012), 31.
3 Regina Lee Blaszczyk, "The Hidden Spaces of Fashion Production" in *The Handbook of Fashion Studies* (London: Bloomsbury Publishing, 2013), 187.

German
Owl Beaker, 1556
Coconut shell and silver with gilding
22.9 × 10.8 × 12.1 cm. (9 × 4 ¼ × 4 ¾ in.)
Gift of Miss Ellen D. Sharpe and
Mrs. Murray S. Danforth 52.533

Double Take

Tara Nummedal /
Eric Anderson

Spring 2016

Manual

Tara Nummedal: A German drinking vessel made out of a coconut, transformed into an owl with the addition of gilt-silver head, feet, wings, and tail. This sort of object conjures up an era in which European rulers defined themselves as much by their learning and mastery of nature as they did by their military prowess. Elites had long prized relics, exotica, and precious stones, of course, valuing them for their material, medical, and sacred virtues. In the Renaissance, however, collectors sought out objects that showcased something new: artifice and ingenuity, whether of humans, nature, or (even better) both at once. The cabinets of curiosity or *Kunstkammern* that housed such items presented visitors with surprising juxtapositions, sparking virtuoso performances of learning and erudition, conversation on the order of the cosmos, and admiration of the wonders of art and nature.

This owl likely nested in just such a collection of a prince or wealthy merchant. Coconuts themselves were prized objects, circulating in Europe since the Middle Ages via trade routes from the East. Collectors especially prized hybrid objects because they demonstrated that artisanal skill could transform already exotic natural materials into something even more spectacular. But the positioning of this owl in a collection might have suggested additional meaning. Perhaps it was placed next to vessels made of rhinoceros horn from India, or seychelles nut

("coco de mer") from the Indian Ocean, highlighting these materials' reputed ability to detect the presence of poison. The owl could also have sat alongside specimens of flying fish, birds, or dragons, inviting a meditation on flight. Or perhaps it alighted atop hunting manuals and other hunting paraphernalia? The small bells attached to the owl's legs suggest a connection to falconry. (Hunting birds often sported such bells so that they could be located once they caught their prey). A coconut, an owl, and a drinking vessel, this beaker offered multiple interpretations, making it a pleasingly complex addition to any good *Kunstkammer*.

A closer look, however, reveals a band around the neck that reads *VERBUM. DOMINI. MANET. IN. [A]ETERNUM 1556* ("The word of the Lord endures forever, 1556"). This phrase became something of a rallying cry for militant Protestant princes, who emblazoned their shields, guns, and banners with the acronym VDMA as they battled the Catholic Emperor Charles V in the 1540s. These wars ended in 1555 with the Peace of Augsburg, which legalized Protestantism and allowed princes to introduce the Reformation to their territories if they wished, a choice that brought enormous institutional, economic, and social transformations as well. If the head of the beaker is removed, a puzzling phrase is revealed: *ALS. ALE. FOEGELEN. SIN. TENIST. SO. IS. DIE. FLEGEN. ANT. ALER. BIST.* This proverb is difficult to decipher in

modern German, but it may have meant something like "Flying is best when all the birds are in their nest" ("Als alle Vögeln zu Nest sind, ist das Fliegen am aller Best"), suggesting another stealthy military tactic.

The owner of this cup, therefore, may well have raised it in a ceremonial toast to the recent military and political victories that granted the Protestant Reformation newfound status in the German lands.

Eric Anderson: **Who says good design necessarily means minimal utilitarianism? This elaborate vessel takes another approach. Instead of paring back, it embraces the possibilities of adding more, combining disparate materials, forms, and uses into a satisfyingly maximal object. The owl beaker consists of two opposed but complementary parts: a simple coconut and finely wrought gilt-silver mountings. The two components are essentially dissimilar in substance and purpose, yet work together in ways that enrich the object visually and expressively, and produce a complex unity.**

As materials, the coconut and metal have been handled in different ways. The woody nut appears more or less as itself. Although husked to remove its fibrous outer skin and polished to enhance its luster, the shell retains visible traces of its organic origins in the irregular striations and mottled brown of the surface. The gilt silver, in contrast, demonstrates a high degree of artifice, having undergone the accumulated labors of mining, refining, gilding, and finishing. An expert artisan, working under the regulations of a guild, cut, bent, hammered, and incised the material to achieve a combination of representational and decorative effects. Much of the smith's effort was given to illustrating the owl's anatomy with convincing naturalism, from the precisely inscribed outlines of the feathers to the wrinkled skin of the toes and the tiny talons. Other parts of the metalwork are structural and decorative: the collar, the vertical straps that cradle the coconut, and the borders around the wings are treated ornamentally with linear, knot-like motifs and a lobed fringe.

The owl beaker, like other figurative cups and jugs of the period, served a dual purpose as useful vessel and object of display.[1] Coconut and metal contributed equally to the utility of the object. The shell, a natural container, held wine or beer; the feet and tail form a tripod base that kept the otherwise wobbly ovoid form upright; and the head provides

Tara Nummedal /
Eric Anderson

both a lid and a cup into which the beverage was poured for drinking. When not being put to occasional use, perhaps in a ceremonial gathering before a hunt,[2] the beaker would have been exhibited in the household of its prosperous owner amid a collection of artistic and natural wonders. The coconut, itself an object of fascination brought from Asia, is appropriately framed for viewing, held up on its fancy pedestal to be admired. At the same time the coconut is transformed by the sculptural mountings into something else entirely—the torso of an owl, to which its shape and coloring are neatly suited. The illusion is enhanced by the hinged, movable wings and the tinkling bells attached to the legs. The little creature seems poised to flap and sing on command, a lively companion ready to entertain. Yet the owl retains a measure of gravity in its masklike face and the religious inscription, which advertises its owner's allegiance to the Protestant Reformation.

Reminding us that there are meanings and pleasures to be found in design beyond less-is-more purity, the owl beaker elevates the quotidian to the delightful and even reverent with its surprising fusion of materials, its formal intricacy, and its communicative richness.

13
/
68

Issue—6

German
Owl Beaker, 1556
Coconut shell and silver with gilding
22.9 × 10.8 × 12.1 cm. (9 × 4 ¼ × 4 ¾ in.)
Gift of Miss Ellen D. Sharpe and Mrs. Murray S.
Danforth 52.533

1 On a similar cup, see Emily Aleev-Snow, "Exploring Coconut Migration Patterns: A Falcon-shaped Standing Cup," *Unmaking Things* 2013/2014, at http://unmakingthings.rca.ac.uk/2014/exploring-coconut-migration-patternsa-falcon-shaped-standing-cup (accessed December 30, 2015).
2 Jonathan Tavares, owl beaker audio commentary, RISD Museum website, http://risdmuseum.org/art_design/objects/408_owl_beaker (accessed December 30, 2015).

Double

Romare Bearden
American, 1911–1988
Ritual, ca. 1965
Collage on board
24.3 × 10.2 cm. (9 9/16 × 4 in.)
Helen M. Danforth Acquisition Fund
2002.31
Art © Romare Bearden Foundation/
Licensed by VAGA, New York, NY

Bob Dilworth /
Leora Maltz-Leca

Take

Spring 2016

Manual

Bob Dilworth: Songwriter, author, poet, musician, organizer, thinker, visionary, dreamer, conceiver of new worlds—throughout his artistic career, Romare Bearden experimented. A personal vernacular realism drove his early works, depicting humanity through various spiritual motifs such as renditions of the Crucifixion of Christ. These experiments continued as he moved into abstraction, using color, line, shape, rhythm, and movement in thin layers of paint, staying true to the expression of humanism and the existence of mankind. Bearden forged an entirely unique visual experience in the early 1960s, when he introduced torn and cut scraps from magazines and other print sources to incorporate into a completely radical, forward-thinking modern aesthetic.

The small collage *Ritual* (1965) belongs to *Prevalence of Ritual*, a series that subverts the limitations placed on African American artists at the time with highly sophisticated arrangements of fractured, stylistic, simple, rhythmic, energized surfaces. A single plane explodes with images, making a subject-specific statement that strikes at the core of modern art and redirects entirely new ideas about African American life.

Bearden was born in North Carolina, and the South claimed him. I grew up in a small rural town in Virginia, and I see *Ritual* as a Southerner at heart and in sentiment. Even if Bearden's entire life were spent elsewhere, he always belonged to the soil, the air, the seasons, and the people of the South. The land of his birth would always be the foundation on which he built all things.

All great works have multiple meanings and unseen forces working behind that which is seen. In *Ritual,* the upper left area becomes a tree laden with fruit. The narrow black trunk defines the left edge; people gather beneath, arms and hands outstretched in an expression of gathering the tree's bounty. As a Southerner, however, I recognize it's not just the seasonal harvest that is implied, but also memories of grandmothers canning vegetables and fruit in Mason jars, of grandfathers picking and hanging tobacco to cure in the tobacco house.

I remember every December 15th, when neighbors gathered to slaughter hogs for the winter, the smokehouse where my father hung large shoulders of ham. These rituals assured that winter would not be met with famine. Southern African American rituals are not simple activities done out of some vague urge to establish cultural continuity and connection, but are necessary activities to sustain life, family, and community.

Certainly one can read broader issues in Bearden's *Ritual* series, but Bearden fiercely tried to distance himself from such connections. He wanted the viewer to focus solely on the realness of his subjects and the amazing collage technique through which he presented them. *Ritual* poses the question, *When you long for something you can never have again, how do you bring back that for which memory is not enough?* The South forever resided in Bearden, and his work will always remain for me a cosmological constant, a philosophical beacon that points to home.

Take

Double

Bob Dilworth /
Leora Maltz-Leca

Leora Maltz-Leca: Under the emerald-teal canopy of a bulbous tree, six cyclops eyes meet our own beholding with equally quizzical stares. Zigzag hands spill out beneath, chasing each other from right to left. And in between this forest of gazing orbs and outsize hands, patches of bodies intervene, sketching the chaos of a crowd. What is this gathering beneath a midnight tree? A supplication? A procession? A ritual of some kind?

Much has been written about the relationship between Bearden's turn to collage in 1964—the year before he made this intimate work—and a concomitant spate of magical titles such as *Conjur Woman* and *Ritual*. Speaking to the latter, Ralph Ellison explained in 1968 how Bearden's postwar Parisian forays instilled an undying interest "in myth and ritual as potent forms for ordering human experience…stepping back from the immediacy of… Harlem."[1] So predominant was the eponymous theme in Bearden's work of the period that his 1971 MoMA retrospective seized on the title *The Prevalence of Ritual* in a nod to the artist's championing of ritual as a universal—and potentially unifying impulse—to be found across cultures and a range of social spheres.

Certainly, Bearden was not alone in this interest. From Joseph Campbell to Adolph Gottlieb, a generation of postwar artists and thinkers all claimed a Jungian legacy that placed myth at the center of art and culture. Politicians saw its potential too. In 1950s Paris, Léopold Senghor and other African nationalists shared Bearden's investment in ritual as an archetypal concept that might help bridge the divide between self and other, which Jean-Paul Sartre and Franz Fanon both located at the heart of racism. From Bearden's standpoint, the way beyond the localism of Harlem life, and the resultant sequestering of black quotidian experience as *raced* experience, lay in tracing nodes of connection with the rest of America: rather than being pigeonholed as a painter of the "black" condition, he might be read as a painter of the *human* condition. Bearden thus deployed ritual to explode the strictures of a narrow gaze that insis-

tently singularizes the experience of the raced other against the universality of the "unmarked" (white, male) subject.

To return, in conclusion, to how Bearden's ritualizing bent relates to his change in medium, it is worth remembering that he initially turned to collage as a potential process of collaborative assemblage: as a promising means by which a group of artists (such as the members of CoBrA) might together create works of political activism. More than anything, what ties Bearden's interest in ritual to his new medium of collage is its potential furthering of timely political concerns, specifically as a universalizing bid against insistent ghettoizing.

This was, of course, both prescient and visionary: a new way of *making* (collage) as well as a new way of *seeing* (via ritual). To this end, perhaps Bearden's flurry of outsize hands, conjoined to a group of enormous eyes, imagines a public of visionary makers and seers. Conjurers, if you will, who are less the traditional perpetrators of rites and rituals than oracles of new American political futures.

1 Ralph Waldo Ellison, "The Art of Romare Bearden," in *The Collected Essays of Ralph Ellison* (New York: Random House, 2003), 692.

Romare Bearden
American, 1911–1988
Ritual (detail), ca. 1965
Collage on board
24.3 × 10.2 cm. (9 9/16 × 4 in.)
Helen M. Danforth Acquisition Fund
2002.31
Art © Romare Bearden Foundation/
Licensed by VAGA, New York, NY

Spring 2016

Manual

F.ROPS.

1

Etching Assemblage

A Collaborative Print from Nineteenth-Century Paris

Britany Salsbury

19
/
68

Issue—6

On a spring evening in 1872, the artists Honoré Daumier, Henri Harpignies, Félicien Rops, and Alfred Taiée attended a party at the Parisian home of the composer and pianist Charles-Wilfrid de Bériot. This informal gathering fostered the collaborative creation of an unusual untitled etching in the RISD Museum's collection that combines five distinct images on the same sheet (Fig. 1). While Bériot played music, the artists passed around a prepared copper plate and took turns sketching into it with a needle.[1] Beyond its literal assemblage of images, the print suggests the multiple types of collaboration— from artist groups to collecting practices—that characterized etching in late nineteenth-century France.

FIGS. 1 and 2
Honoré Victorin Daumier
French, 1808–1879
Alfred Taiée
French, 1820–after 1872
Henri-Joseph Harpignies
French, 1819–1916
Félicien Rops
Belgian, 1833–1898
Etching Study by Four Artists
(detail, opposite), 1872
Etching on paper
Plate: 9.9 × 22.4 cm. (3 7/8 × 8 13/16 in.)
Gift of Mrs. Murray S. Danforth 48.362

DAUMIER.

H. HARPIGNIES.

2

At the time Bériot's party took place, etching was extremely popular among artists because of the ease and expression with which an artist could draw directly on a plate. To produce a print, a wax-coated copper plate is marked with a needle (although some artists were known to use tools like fork tines or toothpicks), and then dipped it into an acid bath so that the lines, left exposed, are incised.[2] The plate is inked, wiped clean, and then run through a press with a sheet of paper, pushing the ink onto the paper and printing the image in reverse. Whereas processes like engraving require carving systematic, regular lines into a plate by hand and the involvement of a skilled craftsperson, etching is similar to drawing, allowing artists to produce prints more independently and outside the studio.

This comparable freedom allowed the RISD Museum's etching to be made as a collaboration in the host's home, rather than at a traditional workspace. The assemblage of images in the etching emphasizes its improvisatory qualities. In the upper center section, for example, Taiée drew a domestic scene where a man—probably Bériot himself—plays a grand piano in a salon decorated with a painting and gaslight while a woman looks on, perhaps assisting with turning the page of his musical score. Taiée created definition and shading with loose parallel strokes of the needle, as seen in the horizontal lines in the background and vertical ones that define the body of the piano. Taiée inscribed the composition along its bottom edge with his signature and the date, noting that the composition was completed "chez Ch. De Bériot." His wobbly script was likely the result of having to write backward for the text to be legible in its printed reversal.

Below Taiée, Harpignies contributed a wooded landscape loosely rendered almost to the point of pure abstraction. A forest is delineated by scribbled lines, on top of which a section of scumbling suggests leaves and grass. In contrast to Harpignies's dense markings, the two sections drawn by Rops seem spare: a woman is shown frontally and in profile using sketched vertical lines and negative space. In the final section, Daumier drew an elderly man, perhaps again their host, who

FIG. 3
Adolphe Martial Potément, called Martial, French, 1828–1883
Cadart & Luquet, publisher
Auguste Delâtre, printer, French, 1822–1907
Headquarters of the Société des Aquafortistes, 1864
Etching
Plate: 29 × 39.3 cm. (11 7/16 × 15 1/2 in.)
Sheet: 35 × 46.7 cm. (13 3/4 × 18 3/8 in.)
The Elisha Whittelsey Collection, The Elisha Whittelsey Fund, 1950
The Metropolitan Museum of Art, metmuseum.org

3

was at that time seventy years old.[3] One corner of the plate remained empty, after the artist to whom it was offered did not complete it.[4] The name of each artist was then inscribed alongside his contribution.

Given their varied interests, experience, and reputations, the four artists who met at Bériot's might seem like an unlikely group of collaborators. By 1872, for example, Daumier had spent a long and prolific career producing political prints and illustrations. A recent transplant from Belgium, Rops was among the most sought-after etchers in Paris for his lightly pornographic subject matter. Harpignies and Taiée were lesser known in comparison, and specialized in rural and urban landscape, respectively. All four, however, were affiliated with an active network, developed over a decade, that encouraged etching and its revival, and, more broadly, original printmaking. This community centered on the Société des Aquafortistes, an organization founded in 1862 by a

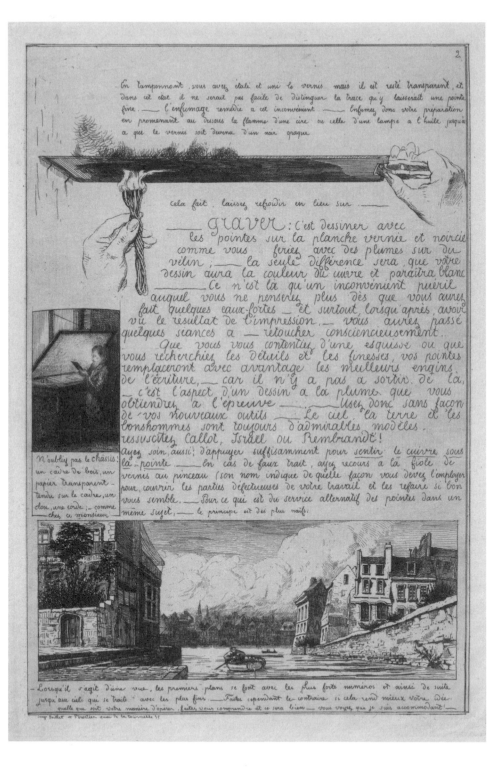

publisher, Alfred Cadart, and printer, Auguste Delâtre. Collaboration was central to the Société's activities, which included sharing technical advice, promoting one another's work through group exhibitions and print albums, and using its headquarters as a gathering place for etchers and enthusiasts (Fig. 3). The four creators of the RISD Museum's print were familiar with this collaborative spirit, as is indicated by Rops's reflection, decades later, that "I made etchings all alone in Belgium, and I was bored to tears [but then a]round 1862, I went to Paris."[5]

In addition to its cumulative format, the RISD Museum's print is indebted to the etching revival not only for its collaborative creation, but also for its sketchy spontaneity and conceptualization directly on a plate. This directness was difficult, if not impossible, in processes such as engraving, which required a composition to be planned carefully in advance. Technical manuals produced by printmakers associated with the Société des Aquafortistes encouraged direct drawing to achieve a free, spontaneous aesthetic. Delâtre, the group's co-founder, described the process, writing that "the artist needs only to take the needle and sketch . . . to improvise his subject."[6] One member of the organization, Maxime Lalanne, authored a widely used guide that described the process similarly, instructing that the etched line "must be free and capricious."[7] Adolphe Martial Potément, another member, combined theory and practice by sketching a didactic text about etching onto a copper plate (Fig. 4): "draw with a needle on a plate . . . like you would with a pen on paper."[8] The RISD Museum's etching was noted early on for this improvisatory quality; in 1886, for example, the print historian Henri Beraldi described it as "five sketches" rather than as a print.[9]

Although the print's proximity to the etching revival helps us to understand its style, fewer precedents explain the social and playful aspects of its creation. The activity of passing around and assembling

FIG. 4
Adolphe Martial Potémont
French, 1828–1883
Letter on the Elements of Etching (page two), 1864
Etching on paper
Plate: 29.7 × 20 cm. (11 11/16 × 7 7/8 in.)
Gift of the Fazzano Brothers 84.198.797

5

a composition may have been a variation on a contemporaneous parlor game, consequences, in which the players write a story together, folding the paper to conceal earlier entries so that all context remained unknown. In the early twentieth century, Surrealist artists appropriated this game and created a cerebral and inventive form of drawing called "exquisite corpse," which involved each artist adding to an existing drawing without seeing the extant composition (Fig. 5).

The work's composition may also have been inspired by Rops, who himself made comparable etchings around this time. In the mid-1860s, he sketched and refined illustrations for Alfred Delvau's journalistic account of Parisian nightlife, *Les Cythères parisiennes, histoire anecdotique des bals de Paris* (1864), on a plate divided into sections almost identical to RISD's print (Fig. 6).[10] The images each show the various nightclubs discussed in the text, and were sketched out on the same plate to conceive of the series as a whole. They were then printed, separated, and bound into copies of the published book. Rops also created etchings he termed *pédagogiques* (teaching tools) by working on the same plate as another artist, to instruct him in technical aspects of the process; in *Bateaux* (Fig. 7), for example, the artist Durand-Brager sketched a boat and Rops contributed several portrait studies. The wide range of marks used in the composition suggests that it was intended to provide Durand-Brager with practice in sketching on the plate. The RISD Museum's print may have had a similarly didactic function, since it was the first and only etching ever produced by Daumier during a career of making nearly four thousand lithographic prints.

FIG. 5
Cadavre Exquis with Yves Tanguy, Joan Miró, Max Morise, Man Ray (Emmanuel Radnitzky), *Nude*, 1926–1927
Composite drawing of ink, pencil, and colored pencil on paper
35.9 × 22.9 cm. (14 ⅛ × 9 in.). The Museum of Modern Art
Digital Image © The Museum of Modern Art/Licensed by
SCALA / Art Resource, NY. © 2015 Artists Rights Society
(ARS), New York / ADAGP, Paris

6

7

FIG. 6
Félicien Rops, Belgian, 1833–1898
Les Cythères parisiennes
(grande planche d'ensemble), ca. 1864
Etching
Sheet: 35.2 × 52.1 cm. (13 ⅞ in x 20 ½ in.)
Image: 23.8 × 34.8 cm. (9 ⅜ in × 13 ¹¹/₁₆ in.)
Mead Art Museum, Amherst College, Massachusetts
Gift of Edward C. Crossett (Class of 1905)/
Bridgeman Images

FIG. 7
Félicien Rops, Belgian, 1833–1898
Durand Brager, French, 1814 –1879
Les Bateaux (Pedagogique)
Etching
Sheet: 31.5 x 45 cm.
Plate: 8.2 x 14 cm.
Digital image © Pierre Bergé &
Associés

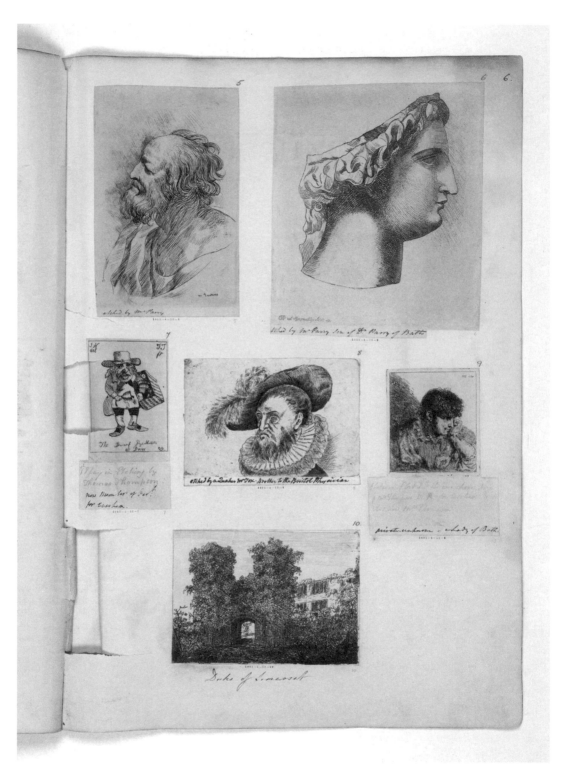

Notably, Rops's *pédagogiques* appealed strongly to contemporary print collectors and fetched especially high prices for their quirky, anecdotal quality.[11] This commercial value helps to explain the fate of the plate made at Bériot's: once finished, Taiée kept it for several years, and it was printed only in 1878, for the catalogue raisonné of Daumier's prints. The etching was added as a frontispiece to each copy of this reference text for collectors, adding value and further appeal. In this context, its composite layout resembles the appearance of a traditional collector's album, into which various prints were compiled (Fig. 8). Just as its inclusion in such an assemblage would have been meant to speak of its owner, the confluence of images, makers, and practice in the RISD Museum's etching illuminates the unique moment within the history of printmaking at which it was made.

1 Champfleury, *Catalogue de l'œuvre lithographié et gravé de H. Daumier* (Paris: Librairie Parisienne, 1878), 47. Historian Janine Bailly-Herzberg has asserted that Taiée had the habit of carrying around copper plates "like [most artists would] a sketchbook," and likely contributed the material; see Bailly-Herzberg, *L'eau-forte de peintre au dix-neuvième siècle, la Société des Aquafortistes (1862–1867)*, vol. 2 (Paris: Leonce Laget, 1972), 64.

2 William M. Ivins Jr., *How Prints Look: Photographs with Commentary* (New York: Metropolitan Museum of Art, 1943), 60.

3 Bailly-Herzberg, *L'eau-forte de peintre au dix-neuvième siècle*, 64.

4 Champfleury, *Catalogue de l'œuvre lithographié et gravé de H. Daumier*, 47.

5 "Je faisais…l'eau-forte tout seul en Belgique et cela m'ennuyait d'en faire mal. –Devers 1862, je vins à Paris…" Félicien Rops, quoted in Anonymous, "Félicien Rops et l'école de gravure en Belgique," *La Plume*, no. 172 (June 15, 1895): 470.

6 "L'artiste n'a plus qu'à prendre la pointe et à tracer sur le vernis le sujet qu'il s'est proposé de graver… improvise ce sujet." Auguste Delâtre, *Eau-forte, pointe sèche et vernis mou* (Paris: Lanier et Vallet, 1887), 10.

7 Maxime Lalanne, *A Treatise on Etching* [1866], trans. S. R. Koehler (Boston: Page Company, 1880), 4.

8 "Graver: c'est dessiner avec les pointes sur la planche…comme vous feriez avec des plumes sur du vélin," Adolphe Martial Potément, *Lettre sur les éléments de la gravure à l'eau-forte* (Paris: Cadart et Luquet, 1864), 1.

9 "…cinq croquis." Henri Beraldi, *Les graveurs du XIXe siècle: guide de l'amateur d'estampes modernes*, vol. 5 (Paris: Librairie Conquet, 1886), 114

10 For details on how these compositions were refined by Rops, see Eugene Rouir, *Félicien Rops, catalogue raisonné de l'œuvre gravé et lithographié*, vol. 2 (Brussels: Claude Van Loock, 1992), 218–19.

11 Rouir, *Félicien Rops*, vol. 2, 69–70.

FIG. 8
Fox
British, active late 18th century
Pasted in volume I of Richard Bull's collection of prints by amateurs, ca. 1805
Etching
9.7 x 14.4 cm.
© The Trustees of the British Museum

Spring 2016

Manual

Assembling History
The Landing of Roger Williams in 1636

Mariani Lefas-Tetenes

Since it was painted in 1857 by artist Alonzo Chappel, *The Landing of Roger Williams in 1636* has instructed generations of adults and school-aged children. This image, its contexts, and its didactic uses provide an opportunity to examine how a historical account from the seventeenth century was used to assemble a narrative that served the politics of nineteenth-century audiences and that still has significant consequences today. By deconstructing the process behind the making of this assemblage, contemporary audiences can grapple with tropes that continue to shape perceptions not only of Roger Williams and Native peoples, but the relationships Americans have with their own national history.

FIG. 1
Alonzo Chappel
American, 1828–1887
The Landing of Roger Williams in 1636 (detail), 1857
Oil on canvas
50.8 × 61.3 cm. (20 × 24 ⅛ in.)
Museum Works of Art Fund 43.003

The painting depicts the moment in which Roger Williams (ca. 1603–1683) and a group of colonists seeking religious freedom arrive along the western shore of the Seekonk River in what is now Rhode Island. However, unlike the way the encounter is presented in the painting, accounts of this event and of the preceding and subsequent months in Williams's life have been pieced together from a variety of incomplete and mythologized sources. We do know that Williams was welcomed by the Wampanoag and Narragansett tribes, and that he learned their language and culture.[1] Chappel groups the figures into distinct areas within the composition: the colonists in the boat are linked by way of Williams's body to the sliver of land on which he stands (Fig. 2). A group of Native people (representing the Narragansett tribe, who welcomed Williams after he was cast out of the Massachusetts Bay Colony) occupies the rest of the land, their collective form extending to and blending with the sky, suggesting pervasive notions of Native peoples' connection to nature and their eventual disappearance as a people[2] (Fig. 3). In contrast to this ethereal characterization, Williams is distinguished by his sturdy pose, enigmatic gesture, and high placement in the center of the scene. The artist has arranged the Native men, women, and children as if they were waiting to welcome the colonists with offerings of food, a bird, and a peace pipe (Fig. 1).

A closer look reveals that the sachem, or leader, and the other Native men wear clothing loosely stereotyping Western Plains Indian warrior attire.[3] Lorén Spears, executive director of the Tomaquag Museum in Exeter, Rhode Island, points out that by the 1800s, "there was propaganda about the Western tribes, and Plains Indians in particular had become the face of all indigenous people," neutralizing the diversity of Native cultures in the United States.[4] The attire and welcoming demeanors of the Native people in Chappel's painting are a stark contrast to the realities of Native people's lives in the 1850s,[5] including those in New England, and reinforce what were already centuries-old notions of the noble savage.[6] The two standing women are draped in textiles and accessorized (Fig. 3), evoking classical references and the myth of the Indian princess, a misconception that ascribed a Eurocentric framework to indigenous societal structures. The children appear cautious and passively waiting, reinforcing

FIG. 2
Alonzo Chappel
American, 1828–1887
The Landing of Roger Williams in 1636, 1857
Oil on canvas
50.8 × 61.3 cm. (20 × 24 ⅛ in.)
Museum Works of Art Fund 43.003

2

the prominence of Williams's arrival and the view of Native peoples as primitives who could be improved by the superior religious and cultural values of European settlers. Colonial narratives like the one in the RISD Museum painting were part of a surge in Pilgrim-themed art that included Longfellow's poetry, Hawthorne's novels, and popular histories such as Bartlett's *The Pilgrim Fathers* (1853).[7]

Chappel painted *The Landing of Roger Williams in 1636* for Jesse Ames Spencer's multi-volume *History of the United States,* first published in 1858.[8] In the mid-nineteenth century, painting and drawings often were made as primary source material to be translated into book illustrations

PAINTED BY ALONZO CHAPPEL.   Martin, Johnson & Company, Publishers, New York.   ENGRAVED BY G. R. HALL.

LANDING OF ROGER WILLIAMS.

4

using the latest steel engraving technology. The richly toned engraving G. R. Hall based on Chappel's painting conveyed subtler effects than had previously been possible (Fig. 4), which was especially appealing to the enterprising publisher Martin Johnson, who sought to amplify the series through this imagery. History volumes lavishly designed and packaged as gift books, often sold by subscription, had become increasingly popular in the 1840s and 1850s, and Chappel contributed to many such histories.

In addition to the engravings used as book illustrations, images related to Chappel's painting of Williams were produced for decorative china and the seal of the City of Providence. This image is still frequently presented in contemporary textbooks, affirming and reinforcing its historical value while perpetuating the notions it presents. Several other images of explorers, settlers, and colonists arriving in the Americas—often welcomed by Native people—appear in Spencer's *History*, reinforcing the dominant Eurocentric imaginary at its heart (Figs. 5, 6, 7, and 8).

Tracing the specific painted or engraved forms that influenced *The Landing of Roger Williams in 1636* is difficult, but the composition supports the idea that the work was assembled from various sources, a common working process for artists of the time. Chappel rarely travelled to study and draw contemporary subjects from life,[9] and he was never in Rhode Island, as far as we know, but it's possible his research for *The Landing* involved reading Romeo Elton's 1853 biography of Williams.[10] Another source Chappel may have been aware of was *The Rhode Island Book: Selections in prose and verse from the writings of Rhode Islanders* (1846), which includes an engraving of Williams's arrival (Fig. 9) that contrasts significantly with Chappel's version. Contemporary historians caution against treating every primary source as a testimonial document, however, particularly when a source deals with events about idealized origins,[11] such as the one Chappel presents. This is especially

FIG. 3
Alonzo Chappel
American, 1828–1887
The Landing of Roger Williams in 1636 (detail), 1857
Oil on canvas
50.8 × 61.3 cm. (20 × 24 ⅛ in.)
Museum Works of Art Fund 43.003

FIG. 4
George R. Hall
American, 1818–after 1857
After Alonzo Chappel
American, 1828–1887
Landing of Roger Williams, 1857
Steel engraving
Image: 14.5 × 18.8 cm.
(5 ¹¹⁄₁₆ × 7 ⅜ in.)
Museum collection 46.476

Spring 2016

Manual

important given the incomplete record of the first interaction between Williams and the Narragansett people who supported his first months in Rhode Island.[12]

To understand Chappel's painting and its appeal, it helps to further situate the image within its original commercial framework, shaped by the publisher, writer, and artists. In the mid-1800s there was a growing market in the United States for pictorial histories that persuasively depicted recent as well as distant events. The engravings paired with these texts were designed to convey ultimate truths in appealing forms. Image and text vied for the attention of the consumer to offer the most powerful historical evidence and capture the imagination.[13]

As idealized pictures of an earlier noble and harmonious American past, *The Landing of Roger Williams* and other engravings in Spencer's *History* were intended to instruct and inspire ordinary nineteenth-century Americans by presenting accounts of noble forebears facing challenging times. To *History*'s readers, exemplars such as Williams must have appeared as especially vital and appealing in the intensifying social and political polarity of the years before the Civil War, and after decades of conflict and violent efforts toward the cultural assimilation of Native American peoples. But while Hall's engraving from Chappel's painting holds a prominent place in the first volume of the series (Fig. 4), Spencer's text about Roger Williams's arrival makes no mention of the moment Chappel depicts, nor does his tone—consistent with his general critical treatment of the Puritans—glorify Williams (Fig. 10). [14]

For nineteenth-century consumers of earlier American history—as well as for us, the subsequent consumers of this pivotal moment—the image persuasively

FIG.5

After Alonzo Chappel, American, 1828–1887

Title page for *History of the United States, Vol. 1*, 1858

Steel engraving

Image: 14.5 × 18.8 cm. (5 ^{11}⁄₁₆ × 7 ⅜ in.)

Museum collection INV2006.549

6

7

8

FIG. 6
After Robert Walter Weir
American, 1803–1889
*Landing of Hendrick Hudson,
from the Original Picture by R. W.
Weir in the Possession of Gulian C.
Verplanck, Esq.*, 1857
Steel engraving
Image: 13.5 × 19 cm. (5 ⅓ × 7 ½ in.)
Museum collection INV2006.549

FIG. 7
John Chester Buttre
American, 1821–1893
After Johannes Adam Simon Oertel
American, b. Germany, 1823–1909
*Elliot, the First Missionary Among
the Indians*, 1856
Steel engraving
Image: 12 × 17.9 cm. (4 ¹¹⁄₁₆ × 7 ¹⁄₁₆ in.)
Museum collection INV2006.549

FIG. 8
George R. Hall
American, 1818–after 1857
After Emanuel Leutze
American, 1816–1868
*English Puritans Escaping to
America, Engraved by Permission
from the Original Painting in the
Possession of Wm. H. Appleton,
Esq.*, ca. 1858
Steel engraving
Image: 13.8 × 17.4 cm. (5 ⅜ × 6 ⅞ in.)
Museum collection INV2006.549

encapsulates Williams's ideals and his legacy of tolerance and fairness.
It perpetuates a harmonious (and still-prevalent) version of the
relationship between the Puritans and the indigenous peoples of New
England, a relationship that, in reality, deteriorated within Williams's
own lifetime and by 1857, when the painting was made, had radically
transformed the cultures of Native peoples throughout New England
and across the United States. We do retain a powerful record of Williams
as an advocate of fair and respectful interactions with Native peoples in
his innovative text *A Key into the Language of America, Or An Help to the*

9

FIG. 9
Louis Fairchild, engraver
American, 1800–after 1840
After Thomas Frederick Hoppin
American, 1816–1872
Landing of Roger Williams, 1846
Engraving
Providence Athenaeum

Language of the Natives in that Part of America called New England (1643).
He is also celebrated as a proponent of religious tolerance, as evidenced
in the Rhode Island state charter, but primary sources that reveal the
perspectives of the Narragansett peoples are rare, if not non-existent.
Many historians and audiences of history continue to value Eurocentric
written and visual sources over the oral histories of indigenous peoples,
affirming the dominant narrative Spencer's *History of the United States*
aimed to convey.

Assembling and interpreting history is a collaborative endeavor, and
spending time with Chappel's image and its layered contexts helps us to
realize that we—like the painter, engraver, writer, and publisher of this
account—choose the sources we use as evidence. Finding new ways to
reframe *The Landing of Roger Williams in 1636* means acknowledging the
inherent constructed nature of historical narratives. Most importantly, it
requires that as readers and viewers, we actively intervene to make visible
repressed or neglected perspectives. While we cannot deny we have been
shaped by dominant historical narratives, paintings such as this one give
us the opportunity to thoughtfully respond to and redress them.

unsettled in judgment, and a troubler of the public peace. It was certainly unfortunate that the scruples of Williams were such as tended to divide and weaken the colony, struggling as it was for independent existence, amid all the difficulties by which it was encompassed. His agitations even served to paralyse resistance against aggressions which they were calculated to bring about: and it must be confessed that, however excellent the principles he had espoused, his conduct bears some tinge of factious opposition, or, to say the least, of an ill-timed and narrow-minded scrupulosity. But his piety was so genuine, and his character so noble and disinterested, that the people of Salem, who knew and loved him, reëlected him for their pastor, in spite of the censure of his doctrines by the Court at Boston, an act of contumacy for which they were reprimanded and punished by the withholding a certain portion of lands. Such harshness aroused Williams to retort by a spirited protest, and he engaged the Salem church to join with him in a general appeal to the other churches against the injustice of which the magistrates had been guilty—a daring proceeding, for which the council suspended their franchise, and they shrunk from their leader, who was thus left absolutely alone. Upon this he openly renounced allegiance to what he deemed a persecuting church. His opinions and conduct were condemned by the council, who pronounced against him a sentence of banishment, but on account of the dangerous feeling of sympathy it awakened, decided shortly after on sending him back to England.

In the depth of a New England winter, Williams fled into the wilderness, and took refuge among the Narragansett Indians, with whom he had become acquainted at Plymouth. He wandered for fourteen weeks through the snow-buried forests, before he reached their wigwams, where he was received and sheltered with the utmost kindness. In the spring he departed in quest of some spot where he could found an asylum for those who, like himself, were persecuted for conscience' sake. He first attempted a settlement at Seekonk, but afterwards, at the friendly suggestion of Winslow, the governor of Plymouth, removed to Narragansett Bay, where he received from the Indians a free grant of a considerable tract of country, and in June, 1636, fixed upon the site of a town, which he named "Providence," as being a refuge from persecution and wanderings. Many of his friends from Salem joined him here, and he freely distributed his lands among them. This was the beginning of the State of Rhode Island, one of the most free and liberal in its institutions of any ever founded in America.

1636.

It was not long before fresh troubles sprang up, in great measure having their origin in the same claim to the right of private judgment in all matters of religious truth and obligation. Hugh Peters, chaplain to Oliver Cromwell, and Henry Vane, a young man of superior ability and acquirements, came over to join the Massachusetts colony. The emigration of a man of Vane's distinction and family created

39 / 68

Issue—6

FIG. 10
Text from page 66 of Spencer's *History of the United States*, Vol. 1 (1858), Museum collection INV2006.549

1 Banished on October 19, 1634, from the Massachusetts Bay Colony, Williams was welcomed and sheltered by Massasoit, a Wampanoag leader, during that first winter. Williams soon received word that because he was still in the territory of the Massachusetts Bay Colony he would be arrested, and so he moved into what is present-day Rhode Island. Williams's flight took place in winter and he was ill. Accounts conflict about whether he was present at the meeting depicted in the painting or if his companions arrived without him at the location on the Seekonk River. For a source that suggests Williams was not present, see Robert A. Geake, *A History of the Narragansett Tribe of Rhode Island: Keepers of the Bay* (Charleston, South Carolina: The History Press, 2011), 16–18. Alternatively, the National Park Service states that Roger Williams was with the group; see http://www.nps.gov/rowi/learn/historyculture/foundingprovidence.htm (accessed January 7, 2016).

2 In an audio recording made July 2, 2015, about Chappel's *The Landing of Roger Williams*, Lorén Spears discussed the detail of "indigenous people morphing into smoke" as an example of the myth of the vanishing Indian, "represent[ing] that erasure of us…. That at some point we are going to drift off into space and become part of the sky and no longer exist." (Recording accessible at http://risdmuseum.org/spears1)

3 This presentation contrasts to the more specific details in clothing and decoration of the young man in another RISD Museum painting, created in the early 1700s, which is devoid of the stereotypical notions of Western Plains Indians that existed in the nineteenth century. Lorén Spears also discussed this painting in a conversation at the RISD Museum on July 2, 2015. (Recording accessible at http://risdmuseum.org/spears2)

American
Native American Sachem, ca. 1700
Oil on canvas
84.1 x 76.5 cm. (33 ⅛ × 30 ⅛ in.)
Gift of Mr. Robert Winthrop 48.246

4 Spears notes that Chappel's *The Landing of Roger Williams* reinforces many myths regarding Native peoples, including those of the noble savage, the Indian princess, and the eco-Indian. (Recording accessible at http://risdmuseum.org/spears1)

5 When Chappel created this painting in 1857, white citizens of the United States were rapidly moving westward, aided by federal policies that relocated Native people to reservations, freeing up their homelands for settlers. A cycle of Native resistance and forced subjugation was played out many times during most of the rest of the nineteenth century. These events are detailed in many historical accounts, including Dee Brown's *Bury My Heart at Wounded Knee: An Indian History of the American West* (1970; repr., New York: Macmillan, 2007).

6 Robert F. Berkhofer, Jr., "European Primitivism, the Noble Savage, and the American Indian," in *The White Man's Indian: Images of the American Indian from Columbus to the Present* (New York: Vintage Books, 1979), 72–80.

7 Barbara Dayer Gallati, "Taste, Art and Cultural Power in Nineteenth-Century America," in *Making American Taste, Narrative Art for a New Democracy*, ed. Dayer Gallati (New York: New-York Historical Society Museum and Library, 2011), 83.

8 *History of the United States* was an ambitious publication. Publisher Martin Johnson was aiming to improve on significant recent pictorial histories, including John Frost's four-volume *Pictorial History of the United States* (1844) and Benson J. Lossing's *Pictorial Field-Book of the Revolution* (late 1840s).

9 David Meschutt, "Portraits by Alonzo Chappel," in *The Portraits and History Paintings of Alonzo Chappel* (Chadds Ford, Pennsylvania: Brandywine River Museum, 1992), 19.

10 Romeo Elton was a professor of Greek and Latin languages at Brown University in Providence, as discussed by Adelaide M. Budde in "The Landing of Roger Williams by Alonzo Chappel," *Museum Notes, Museum of Art, Rhode Island School of Design* 2, no. 2 (February 1944): 12.

11 Keith C. Barton, "Primary Sources in History: Breaking through the Myths," in *The Phi Delta Kappan* 86, no. 10 (June 2005): 745–53.

12 Robert A. Geake, *A History of the Narragansett Tribe of Rhode Island*, 16–18.

13 For an extensive and relevant analysis of pictorial histories in the United States, see Gregory M. Pfitzer, *Illustrated Histories and the American Imagination: 1840–1900* (Washington and London: Smithsonian Institution Press, 2002), specifically chapter 3, on the context and production of Spencer's *History*, "'Vulgar and Strict Historical Truth': Giftbooks, Sentimental History, and the Grand Manner," 65–96.

14 For Spencer's treatment of Puritans, see a short discussion by Gregory M. Pfitzer at http://www.cliohistory.org/visualizingamerica/picturingpast/part-two/three-way-collaborations/englishpuritans/ (accessed December 28, 2015). For a more in-depth discussion of Spencer's motivations, see Pfitzer, 74–76.

Portfolio

objects are identified on page 66

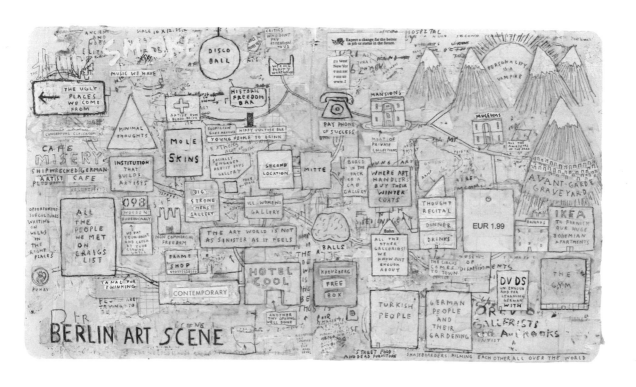

Spring 2016

Manual

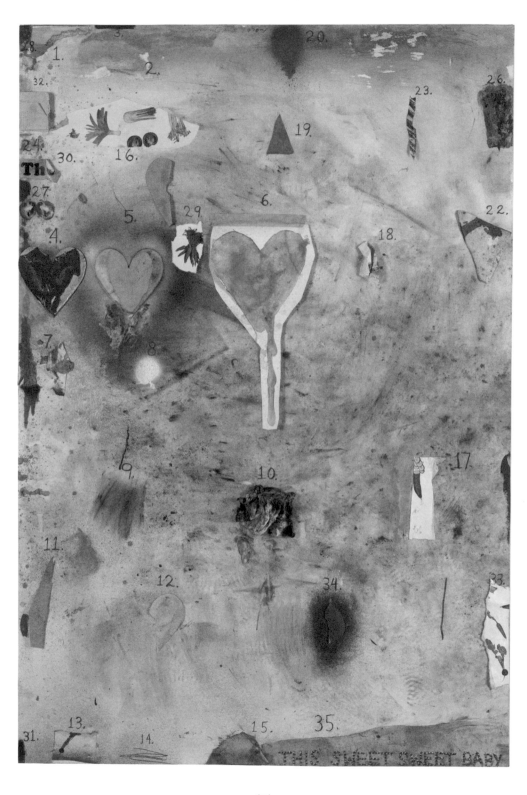

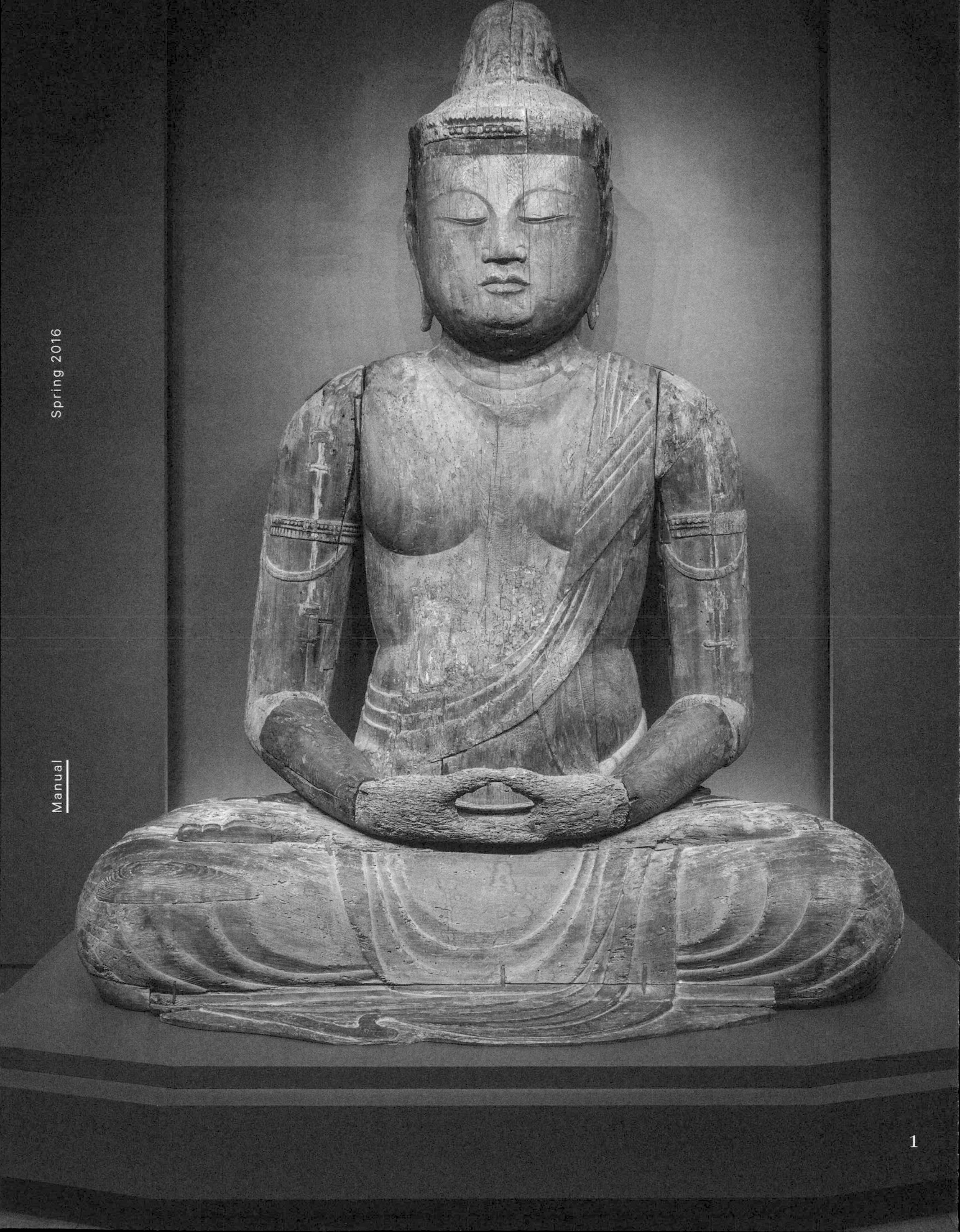

Learning from the Buddha

The Conservation of a
Multipart Japanese Wooden Figure

Ingrid A. Neuman

53 / 68

A late Heian period Japanese Buddha has been in residence on the sixth floor of the Rhode Island School of Design Museum for eighty years. More than nine feet high and seven feet wide, it is a majestic sculpture (Fig. 1) which sits in solitude in a dedicated space that was renovated in 2014. Over many decades, the RISD Buddha has become an iconic image, drawing generations of visitors to seek quiet moments in its daunting yet serene presence. The figure's downward gaze is prevalent in twelfth-century sculptures of the Buddha,[1] and the wide and shallow parallel bands of carved drapery on the lap and chest are associated with a style developed by Jōchō, the highly admired and frequently imitated sculptor who worked during the first half of the eleventh century. The unidentified sculptor of the RISD Buddha appears to have emulated Jōchō's style (Fig. 3). Although Buddha sculptures abound in museum collections throughout the world, this sculpture is highly unusual in the United States for its age, scale, and composition.[2]

Issue—6

FIG. 1
Japanese
Buddha Mahavairocana (Dainichi Nyorai),
ca. 1150–1200
Cryptomeria wood
294.6 × 212.1 × 165.1 cm. (116 × 83 ½ × 65 in.)
Museum Appropriation Fund 36.015

The Buddha was originally delivered in January 1935 to the Museum of Fine Arts in Springfield, Massachusetts, but an undocumented set of serendipitous circumstances soon led Yamanaka & Co. to offer it for purchase to RISD Museum director L. Earle Rowe,[3] and the Buddha came to reside on the sixth floor of the RISD Museum prior to February 24, 1936. Established in 1894, Yamanaka & Co. was one of the first art dealers to import Asian antiquities to America, selling to early collectors who contributed to the Asian collections at the Metropolitan Museum of Art, the Boston Museum of Fine Arts, and the Harvard Art Museums, to name a few.[4] Yamanaka & Co. thoroughly documented their daily business transactions, however the company was dissolved during World War II as a result of Executive Order No. 9095,[5] and it is now difficult to trace the roots of this sculpture.[6] The original sales receipt does not state where the sculpture originated, referring to it as the "Fujiwara wood carved seated Dainichi Nyorai YR 5258 which was to be sent by wagon" from Springfield to the RISD Museum.[7]

FIG. 2
RISD Buddha before conservation treatment

FIG. 3
Jōchō Busshi, Japanese, d. 1057
Amida Nyorai Buddha, 1051
Phoenix Hall of Byodoin Temple, Kyoto, Japan

2

3

The RISD Buddha is composed of *Cryptomeria Japonica*, a wood commonly referred to as Japanese cedar (*Sugi*) but technically from the cypress family. The use of wood surpassed the use of bronze in sculpture production during the Heian period, but wooden sculptures, composed of solid timber, were limited in size to the tree's dimensions. However, from the mid-tenth century until the mid-twelfth century, an innovative construction technique known as *yosegi-zukuri* allowed for smaller blocks to be joined together. This additive process led individual sculptors to specialize in different body parts. It also allowed greater portability of whole sculptures (which by this time were hollow and lighter in weight), at the same time improving dimensional stability and reducing cracking and warping. Because of specialization within this new process, the proportions for individual parts may have become more standardized during this time. Wood can be a more vulnerable construction material than metal, so this pre-fabricated system also made it easier to make replacement parts when needed.[8] The yosegi-zukuri composition

4   5

technique is clearly visible when examining the RISD Buddha, which
is composed of eleven components made up of more than thirty parts,
some of which appear to be replacements. The use of so many pieces of
wood to compose a sculpture is particular to Japan, and is not common
in sculpture from other Asian countries or Europe.[9]

Constructed with square mortise and tenons, the RISD Buddha is
carved in the round, which may indicate it was originally meant to be
viewed from all sides. The two-part hollow head inserts into the neck,
and the multipart hollow torso assemblage locks into the hip and lap
unit, which is also multipart and hollow. The front piece of drapery
appears to be a later restoration. Many of the individual wooden blocks
are secured with iron hardware called *kasugai.* These originally would
have been inset within the wood so they were flush with the surface of
the carving (Fig. 4) and secured in place with a lacquer paste known as
kokusou-urushi.[10] Replacement kasugai added later are clearly visible
above the carved wooden surface[11] (Fig. 5). The kasugai on the interior
are also most likely later additions, possibly from when it was reassem-
bled and an interior armature added for support after it arrived at the
RISD Museum in 1936 (Fig. 6).

What is somewhat perplexing to admirers of this colossal Buddha
is the difference in the surface quality of the wooden components.
Although Japanese cedar was confirmed to be present throughout the
sculpture, the visual appearance of the wood of the forearm versus

FIG. 4
Detail of inset *kasugai*

FIG. 5
Replacement kasugai, added later
and visible above the surface

Issue—6

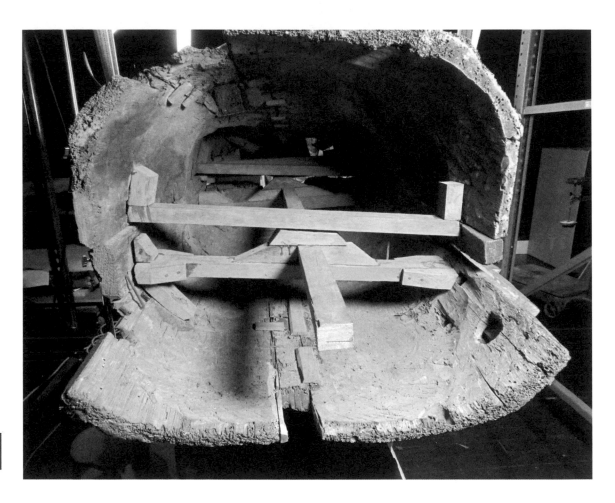

7

8

Issue—6

the wood of the hands is quite apparent.[12] It appears that the surface degradation is the result of wood-boring insect attack and, possibly, water erosion (Fig. 7). Both powderpost and deathwatch beetles are common attackers of this wood.[13]

Although no restoration or conservation treatment is recorded between 1936 and 2013, earlier historic restorations can be observed in both forearms, the left big toe, the left knee, and the front drapery (Figs. 7 and 8). Less obvious is the restoration of the hair, which appears to be pigmented black paper (Fig. 9). All this work most likely occurred in the post-Edo (1600–1868) or Meiji period (after 1868). In the Heian period, hair more typically would have been painted using *gunjyo,* a pigment ground from the mineral lapis lazuli.[14] It is not unusual for historical restorations to be visible on older sculptures. These features are thought-provoking, providing evidence of ever-changing cultural attitudes regarding preservation.

Originally, this sculpture most likely would have been lacquered and gilded, a much more polished surface than the carved bare wood we see today.[15] Unfortunately, it appears that more than eight hundred years of history have removed most traces of this original surface finish, possibly through exposure to the elements in an open-air temple. While some lacquer appears to be visible on the lap area under the proper left forearm, the majority of what we can see with the naked eye is an

FIG. 6
Internal armature, added in 1936

FIG. 7
Detail of hands and drapery before treatment

FIG. 8
Detail of previously restored large toe

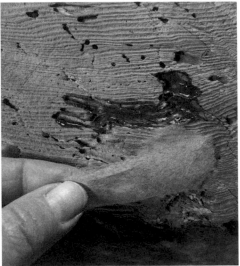

9   10

unadorned wooden surface and the historical details of the sculpture's construction, preservation, and restoration. The visual discrepancy between the condition of the forearms and the hands, for instance, is the difference between the formerly restored sections and the original sections of the sculpture. This presents a most perplexing question: *Why were the forearms replaced, but not the structurally degraded and weakened hands* (Fig. 7)?

In 2014, the conservation treatment on the Buddha involved the selection of stable materials applied in a reversible fashion, as is mandated in contemporary Western philosophies of art conservation. In this case, cleaning conducted with compressed air allowed for minimal contact with the degraded wooden surface. Minimal and reversible cosmetic visual improvements were performed using neutral-pH Japanese paper toned with gouache, affixed with a stable methylcellulose adhesive applied by brush (Fig. 10). The applications of toned paper were limited to the most severely degraded areas, where the original wood carving was no longer clearly visible. In keeping with the tenets of Western art conservation, which emphasize stabilization over restoration, missing areas such as the left ear lobe were not restored (Fig. 11), as the entire right ear lobe is extant and therefore serves an example for study.

FIG. 9
Detail of an earlier restoration of the hair

FIG. 10
Toned Japanese paper is secured with methylcellulose during conservation treatment

FIG. 11
Detail of the missing portion of the proper left earlobe

11

Despite centuries of degradation and multiple restorations, it is clear that this Buddha is of significant importance. In a letter dated February 24, 1936, Tanaka Kichijiro, a salesperson at Yamanaka & Co.'s New York store, then located at 680 Fifth Avenue, wrote to the director of the RISD Museum, "It is one of the most important sculptures we have ever brought over from Japan of late and, no doubt, there is no question about it being adopted as a national treasure if we ever return it to Japan, and I sincerely hope that your Museum will be able to retain it as a permanent possession."[16]

1 William Watson, *Sculpture of Japan: from the Fifth to the Fifteenth Century* (New York: Viking, 1959), 34.

2 See the list of the National Treasures of Japan (Sculptures), available in Japanese at http://kunishitei.bunka.go.jp/bsys/searchlist.asp (accessed December 30, 2015); it appears the largest known Heian wooden Buddha sculpture is approximately four inches smaller than the RISD Buddha.

3 K. Tanaka, letters to L. Earle Rowe dated January 21 and November 16, 1935, and February 24 and March 4, 1936, RISD Museum Archives.

4 Yuriko Kuchiki, "The Enemy Trader: The United States and the End of Yamanaka," *Impressions: The Journal of the Japanese Art Society of America* 34 (2013): 33–53.

5 Issued by Franklin D. Roosevelt in 1942, Executive Order No. 9095 established the Office of the Alien Property Custodian, which oversaw and heavily restricted Japanese business dealings in the United States.

6 Ibid.

7 K. Tanaka, letter to L. Earle Rowe dated March 4, 1936, RISD Museum Archives.

8 I. Nagasawa, T. Shida, and H. Oshima, "Polychrome Wooden Buddhist Sculptures in Japan: History, Materials and Techniques," ICOM Committee for Conservation (1999): 434–36.

9 Kyotaro Nishikawa, "Conservation of Wooden Sculpture," Proceedings, ISCRP, Wood Conservation (1983): 141.

10 Marianne Webb, *Lacquer: Technology and Conservation* (Oxford, U.K.: Butterworth-Heinemann, 2000), 26.

11 Fujimoto Seiichi, of the Bijutsuin National Treasure Studio, in a letter to the author dated November 30, 2014.

12 R. Bruce Hoadley, professor emeritus at the University of Massachusetts, Amherst, in a wood identification analysis dated March 5, 2014.

13 Hisayuki Onodera, "The Repair of Wood Sculptures," Proceedings, ISCRP, Wood Conservation (1983): 147–48.

14 Fujimoto Seiichi, of the Bijutsuin National Treasure Studio, in a letter to the author dated November 30, 2014.

15 Ibid.

16 K. Tanaka, letter to L. Earle Rowe dated February 24, 1936, RISD Museum Archives.

Further Reading

Kakiuchi, Emiko. "Cultural Heritage Protection System in Japan: Current Issues and Prospects for the Future," National Graduate Institute for Policy Studies, Tokyo, Japan, discussion paper 14-10, July 2014, 2–12.

Kurata, Bunsaku. "Conservation of Wooden Sculptures in Japan," Proceedings International Symposium on the Conservation and Restoration of Cultural Property, Tokyo National Research Institute of Cultural Properties (1978), 67–75.

Okamura, Yuki. "The Japanese Art Dealer Yamanaka Sadajiro: His New York City Period, 1893–1936," Fashion Institute of Technology graduate thesis, 2003.

How To

Make a Capri Battery: *Come on Beuys, Shine*
by Christina Hemauer and Roman Keller

Joseph Beuys
German, 1921–1986
Capri Battery, 1985
Lightbulb with plug socket, screenprinted
wooden box, offset lithograph on paper, lemon
8 × 16 × 6 cm. (3⅛ × 6⁵⁄₁₆ × 2⅜ in.)
Gift of James Baker 2008.66

The *Capri Battery* of Joseph Beuys (1921–1986) is considered a modern metaphor for the ecological balance of civilization. 200 pieces were manufactured as a limited edition in 1985. The vitrine, in which Beuys displayed a *Capri battery*, is considered to be one of his last works before he died. Twenty years later, this guide serves to get the Capri Battery to work.

«COME ON BEUYS, SHINE», *ROMAN KELLER, 2005**

1. MATERIALS
Lemon, yellow lightbulb, yellow high-performance LED (2.4 V, 20 mA), screw (M4, 20 mm) with washer screw nut, luster terminal (hole diameter: 3.5 mm), lamp socket E27, 15 cm copper wire, 15 cm magnesium wire, 2 × 10 cm copper cord 1.5 m2.

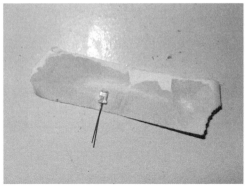

4. SANDING THE TOP PART OF THE LED
In order that the arising light doesn't come out at the top of the LED, you should sand the top of the LEDs head (diffusing its light).

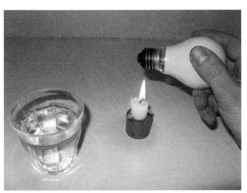

2. HEATING UP THE SOCKET OF THE LIGHTBULB
Heat up the socket of the lightbulb with a candle or a gas burner.

5. CUTTING OFF THE SPIRAL-WOUND FILAMENT
Cut off the spiral-wound filament and the associated supporting wires of the lightbulb with an edge cutter.

3. SEPARATING THE SOCKET OF THE LIGHTBULB
Cool down the socket by shocking it in a glass of ice water. The glass of the lightbulb should split near the socket.

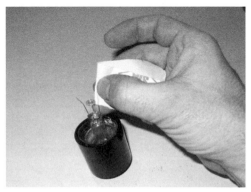

6. SANDING THE CONTACTS
To simplify the soldering of the LEDs you should sand the contacts first (otherwise the solder won't bind properly with the contacts).

7. ISOLATE AND MOUNT LED CONTACTS
Isolate the LED contacts at the bottom with a short piece of insulating tape. After that, fix the LED in the round opening in the middle between the two contacts.

8. SOLDERING THE LED
Solder the LED with a soldering tool to the contacts that used to hold the spiral-wound filament.

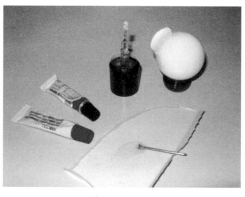

9. GLUE THE LIGHTBULB TOGETHER
Use some two-component adhesive (e.g., Araldit) to glue the bulb together.

10. COMPLETED LIGHTBULB WITH EMBEDDED LED

11. ASSEMBLING THE SOCKET
The M4 screw is used to hold together the E27 lightbulb socket with the luster terminal.

12. ASSEMBLING THE ELECTRODES
Put the copper and magnesium wires (alternating) into the luster terminal. The middle wires are connected at the back side with a short piece of flexible wire.

13. ATTACHING THE LEMON
The lemon is attached orthogonally to the wires.

14. BOTTOM VIEW
Here you can see the final design from the bottom.

15. OPERATING TEST
As the power capacity of the lemon battery is very low, the LED will emit only a pale, subdued shine. You can see it best in a dark room or cupboard.

Portfolio

(1)
Quilt, ca. 1887
American
Pieced, embroidered, and painted silk velvet
and satin
195.6 × 175.3 cm. (77 × 69 in.)
Gift of Mrs. Patricia Barrett 80.280

(2)
Simon Evans
English, b. 1972
Berlin Art Scene, 2009
Collage with pen and ink, correction fluid,
and tape on paper
Sheet: 25.2 × 44.1 cm. (9 15/16 × 17 3/8 in.)
Richard Brown Baker Fund for Contemporary
British Art 2009.86
© Simon Evans

(3)
Roman
Portrait of Agrippina the Younger, ca. 40 CE
Ancient head: Marble (from Paros)
Bust and base: 18th-century colored-marble
Height: 81.6 cm. (32 1/8 in.)
Anonymous gift 56.097

(4)
Meredith Stern
American, b. 1976
Through the Looking Glass Ceiling, 2014
Collage with linocut, woodcut, spray paint, and ink
on paper
Sheet: 75.8 × 57.4 cm. (29 13/16 × 22 5/8 In.)
Museum purchase: Gift of Joseph A. Chazan, MD
2014.68.2
© Meredith Stern

(5)
Ryan Trecartin
American, b. 1981
Lizzie Fitch
American, b. 1981
Take a Stand, 2006
Books; mesh bag with twigs, rocks, reed flowers,
human hair; papier mâché; wood; fabric; deodorant
stick; rubber; microphone; cinder blocks; box cutter;
plastic; paint; and glue
228.6 × 182.9 × 198.1 cm. (90 × 72 × 78 in.)
Phil Seibert Alumni Acquisition Fund and Helen M.
Danforth Acquisition Fund 2008.3
© Ryan Trecartin and Lizzie Fitch

(6)
Jim Dine
American, b. 1935
This Sweet Sweet Baby, 1970–1971
Collage and mixed media on paper
Sheet: 152.4 × 101 cm. (60 × 39 13/16 in.)
Museum purchase with funds from the National
Endowment for the Arts 71.070
© 2015 Jim Dine / Artists Rights Society (ARS),
New York

(7)
Robert Rauschenberg
American, 1925–2008
Horsefeathers Thirteen XIV, 1972
Lithograph, screenprint, collage, and embossing
Sheet: 65.9 × 51.5 cm. (25 7/8 × 20 5/16 in.)
Museum purchase with funds from the National
Endowment for the Arts 74.011
Art © Robert Rauschenberg Foundation/Licensed
by VAGA, New York, NY

(8)
Attributed to William B. Savage
American, active 1880–1890
Spinning-Wheel Armchair, ca. 1886
Red oak, basswood, and buttonwood
99.1 × 48.3 × 48.3 cm. (39 × 19 × 19 in.)
Gift in memory of Nathalie Lorillard Bailey Morris
by Elizabeth Morris Smith 78.157

(9)
Christo
American, b. 1935
*300 Wrapped Trees (Project for Avenue des
Champs-Élysées - Paris)*, 1969
Pencil, wax crayon, polyethylene, twine, staples,
photographs, map, and tape on board
Sheet: 71.1 × 55.9 cm. (28 × 22 in.)
Gift of Mr. and Mrs. Herbert C. Lee 78.221
© Christo

(10)
Vlisco, manufacturer
Dutch, 1846–present
Obama, 2008
Cotton; wax printed
Length: 120 × 548.6 cm. (47 1/4 × 216 in.)
Georgianna Sayles Aldrich Fund 2009.68.2
© The Vlisco Group